POETRY OF HEALTHCARE
AND COMPASSION

PROFESSOR PATRICK PIETRONI

FRESCO BOOKS

CONTENTS

4   *My Mind Lets Go a Thousand Things*
     Helen Urquhart

7   INTRODUCTION

8   INTRODUCTORY OVERVIEW
     OF HEALTHCARE SYSTEMS

     9   Factors Determining Healthcare Systems

     9   Comparison of Relationship Between Primary
          and Secondary Care Systems

11   DISEASE, ILLNESS, SICKNESS AND HEALTH

     11   *Say Not the Struggle Nought Availeth*
           Arthur Hugh Clough

17   NOW WHAT ABOUT HEALTH?

     17   *On the Physical State of Beiing*
           J R Curtin

     18   What is Health?

22 COMPASSION AND THE DELIVERY
OF HEALTHCARE IN PRIMARY CARE

    23 *Doctors*
    Rudyard Kipling

30 COMMUNITY ORIENTED
PRIMARY HEALTHCARE

    30 The Consultation

    36 The Responsiveness of the Practice/Doctor's Office

    41 Outreach and Community Care

    43 The Patient Journey In and Out of Hospital

44 FINALLY

    44 *The Shropshire Lad: II – Loveliest of Trees*
    The Cherry Now
    A E Housman

45 COMPASSION WITHIN HEALTHCARE SETTINGS

MY MIND LETS GO A THOUSAND THINGS

Like dates of wars and deaths of kings
And yet recalls the very hour
Twas noon by yonder village tower.

The wind came crisply up the bay

To Thomas Bailey Aldrich's poem, I take great license by adding
my own lines ...

And then he arrived
Like spindrift from another sea
That will long remember
Bringing a gestalt of feelings and experiences.

It began with the way you remind me of a leprechaun
Smiling mischievously
As your eyes light up and twinkle
Dimming their frame of ruddy hair.

You did bring with you hidden treasures!
Those of feelings
Which you slowly seeded
Risking that the soil could be tilled.
Patiently waiting
Carefully proceeding
The known and the knowing.
It was magic to watch!

Blessed are those who can sow new beginnings
So we may have seeds for our gardens.
And blessed are those who accept the harvest
To learn that the person to person realationship
        (a typo I deliberately love to make!)
Can be a personal venture
A journey together
To a place where
The patient becomes
"Another person like me".

The endless process of being and becoming
As we respond to another's feelings
And become freer
And freer
And freer.

And as another responds to our feelings
Together we both are free
From the forged chains of indifference
Though only we may know
They have been broken
As I feel you did for me.

You are, in my mind, like
The American, Johnny Appleseed,
Who scattered apple seeds
As he traveled this country
For that purpose.

He, too had many treasures to plant!
The apple trees grew and bore fruit
To enjoyably nurture many
Stout trunks provided rest for weary bodies
And respite under massive shade
From sun-scorched manual labor
Children played and climbed in their strong arms
And lovers made vows under their arbor
Leaving symbols carved in bark
To mark the feelings
And as soft spring winds carried the fragrance
Of pink and white apple blossoms
They heralded that new beginnings
Were felt upon the land.

Like the leprechaun's, Johnny Appleseed's treasures
Were a tribute to man to nature
Perhaps unattended by some
Taken for granted by others
For the messages are subtle.

You also remind me of words from Gibran who wrote,
"… Should you sit upon a cloud you would not see
    the boundary line between one country and another"
Just as Johnny Appleseed did not see from his cloud,
"… The boundary line between a farm and a farm".

Helen Urquhart [1]

INTRODUCTION

The first six volumes of this series covered:
Vol. I   – The Poetry of Compassion
Vol. II   – Poetry and the Science of Compassion
Vol. III – The Poetry of Global Compassion
Vol. IV – Poetry and the Education of Compassion
Vol. V   – Poetry and the Psychology of Compassion
Vol. VI – Poetry and the Evolution of Compassion
Vol. VII– Poetry of Morality, the Religions and Compassion

The framework of these short volumes allows the reader to have an introduction to the specific focus of the book. They are accompanied by poems and images that help to add an aesthetic and emotional experience.

This eighth volume focusses on why the concept of compassion is so important in our healthcare system and what can be done to restore its centrality in the doctor/patient encounter.

INTRODUCTORY OVERVIEW OF HEALTHCARE SYSTEMS

In this time of the Covid-19 pandemic it can be helpful to review how healthcare systems across the world have evolved. What are the factors that will ensure compassion remains central to the experience of being a patient, or should we now be saying "customer"?

The three following tables summarise much of what has been written on the subject.

A. Factors Determining Healthcare Systems

Factors determining healthcare systems

1. Cultural and Population Needs
2. Ideological and Political
3. Funding and Finance
4. Managerial and Organisational
5. Professional and Clinical
6. Educational and Research
7. Leadership: Top-down/Bottom-up
8. Change Management

B. Comparison of Relationship Between Primary and Secondary Care Systems

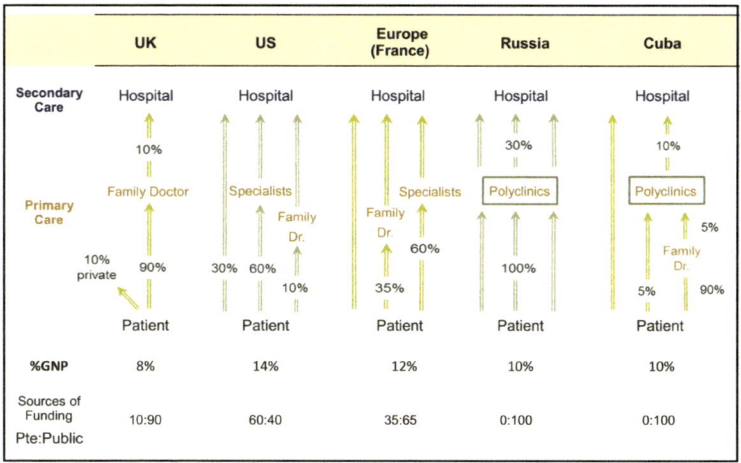

It is important to remember that all cultures have three 'loose' systems of healthcare (self-care, folk care and professional care), and that as the next table suggests, only a small proportion of our citizens seek out professional care.

What People Do About Their Symptoms

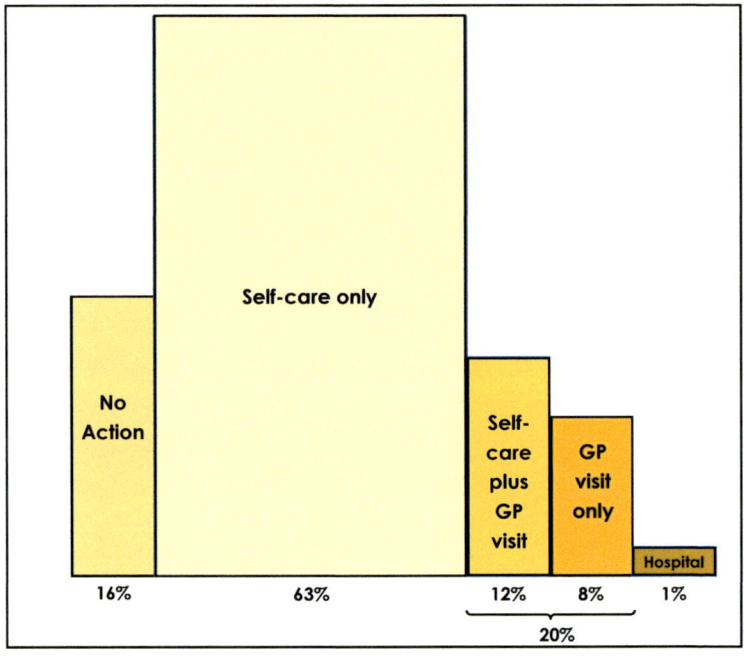

SAY NOT THE STRUGGLE NOUGHT AVAILETH

Say not the struggle nought availeth,
*   The labour and the wounds are vain,*
The enemy faints not, nor faileth,
*   And as things have been they remain.*

If hopes were dupes, fears may be liars;
*   It may be, in yon smoke concealed,*
Your comrades chase e'en now the fliers,
*   And, but for you, possess the field.*
For while the tired waves, vainly breaking
*   Seem here no painful inch to gain,*
Far back through creeks and inlets making,
*   Comes silent, flooding in, the main.*

And not by eastern windows only,
*   When daylight comes, comes in the light,*
In front the sun climbs slow, how slowly,
*   But westward, look, the land is bright.*

Arthur Hugh Clough [2]

COGITO ERGO SUM

DISEASE, ILLNESS, SICKNESS AND HEALTH

I use these four terms because it is important to understand their difference in each encounter with "the patient". I digress with a "short" history of Western Medicine.

By the time of Copernicus's death in 1543, his *Revolution of the Celestial Bodies*[3] was already fueling the first of debates initiated by Lutheran reformism. New thinking was dangerous, even heretical. To suggest that the earth revolved around the sun not only weakened the authority of the Church but suggested that knowledge was attainable through reasoned thought as distinct from ecclesiastical teaching or divine revelation.

As Galileo was establishing the proof of the Copernican hypothesis, Descartes was laying the foundations for rational scientific enquiry. His famous dictum, *"I think, therefore I am"*, [4] was particularly significant in that he was confirming the march of Reason through territory traditionally dominated by ecclesiastical authority. Man was beginning to free himself from the dogma of the Church and preparing the ground for a new kind of authority – rational science.

By the time of the publication of Newton's *Principia*[5] in 1687, few vestiges of the "old world" remained. The "celestial orbs" moved through space in perfect defined motion. Life was no longer "nasty, brutish and short", as Hobbes[6] had described it sixty years earlier. Descartes' philosophical dualism had separated the physical from the metaphysical, and hence mind from body and Man from God. In his search for a unified philosophy whereby men would become "masters and possessors of nature", Descartes broke with the imprecise and occult traditions of mediaeval science to pursue a universally applicable method of establishing verifiable knowledge. It was not that he sought to reject metaphysics or the use of Pure Reason, rather that he doubted the veracity of their employment. Better to start from a position of skepticism, he argued, and to deduce answers from logical formulae, than to assume the Mind as being capable of independently verifying universal truths.

Whether or not Descartes is responsible for the mistakes that science has made in respect to Man and Nature over the past three hundred years cannot obscure the fact that it was his systematic method that gave rise to the *mechanistic, reductionist* and *dualistic* concepts that have since become the hallmarks of rational-scientific enquiry. "I consider the human body as a machine", he wrote. "My thought compares a sick man and an ill-made clock with my ideas of a healthy man and a well-made clock. I say that you consider these functions occur naturally in this machine solely by the dispositions of its organs not less than the movement of a clock". [7]

Most medicine and most of my teaching as a doctor focused on how those bits work. Very rarely were we actually taught how those parts came together and how they function together as a whole. Most of medicine has been reductionistic, and has been about identifying the flaw in the part rather than looking for the relationship between the parts: between how the heart and the skin might relate to each other, or whether the mind and the bones might be linked, or whether the atmosphere and what you breathe in might have something to do with a skin rash that you have, and so on. Those kinds of issues and their connections weren't something that I was taught. I was taught to look at things discretely and analytically, and to separate them out, to keep them separate and study them separately. That is the reductionistic model.

Now it seems to me that when you go to a doctor or when you seek help for a particular problem the doctor has a number of different levels that he needs to address. One is clearly, "Well, what is the *disease* that his person has? What is the part that is not functioning?" And it could be the heart, could be the skin, could be the joints or whatever. But he has a much greater task than that. As I understand it, *disease* is the way that parts function or don't function. *Illness* is what we ourselves make of our *diseases*. Let me give you an example. If I have a cold or if any of us has a cold, the part that's not functioning is my lungs and my nose and my mouth and I can tell you the cells that are inflamed and the viruses that caused it. That's the *disease* of having a cold. But what's the *illness* of having a cold? It could be anything: "Pass me my bottle of Scotch. I'm not going into work today. I'm going into see the doctor. I need some antibiotics. I want a certificate off work". That is the *illness*. It is the personal response to the *disease*. At the other extreme, two people with a heart attack may have the same enzyme changes and the same electrocardiographic changes. One might deny it completely and say "Well look, I'm not going to pay any attention to this chest pain, I'm going to continue to work." The other might be terrified and frightened and not want to go out of the house. That is the *illness* of the heart attack.

We may not have as much control over the *diseases* that we are going to experience in our lives, but we do construct our own *illnesses* and that's where the issue of responsibility, I think, comes in. There is a mistake that is often made in this issue of responsibility in healthcare. People may have little responsibility for their *diseases*, but they may have much more responsibility for their *illnesses*. One has to begin to separate that out in working with his/her level of Response Ability, ie *ability to respond*.

Now, *sickness* is a little bit more complex. If I have a cold, we've talked about the *disease* which is in the upper respiratory tract and have talked about my personal response to my *disease*. But what about my wife's response to my *illness*? What about my boss's response to my *illness*? What about my community's response to my *illness*? What often can make people sick is the reaction that other people have to their own *disease*.

Doctors unfortunately find themselves busying away trying to treat the *disease*, when really they should be responding to the *illness*. Most of the time people bring to them their sickness – their sense of isolation, their sense of lack of support, their sense of not being understood by their close family and friends and comforters.

We are living through the Covid-19 pandemic which is a perfect example of how the *disease* may be fatal or indeed may be non-symptomatic. The *illness* will almost certainly include fear, the isolation from close family and the impact on family members. We are also witnessing the *"sickness"* of those unaffected by the illness who have lost their jobs or developed stress related symptoms which have led to mental health disorders (increases in divorces, physical abuse and anti-social behaviours).

NOW WHAT ABOUT HEALTH?

ON THE PHYSICAL STATE OF BEING

*Our physical state of being controls our mobility,
our strength, and our physical fitness.
A healthy physical body needs a coupling
with a healthy mind to reach its potential.
A positive or negative reaction
to our own physical state, including any
disabilities or frailties, and the
reaction of others toward our state
can be a force for our empowerment or
continued frustration.*

*Controlling the physical state of being
is not always possible, but presenting
a positive attitude is not only possible,
but essential for well-being. Adapting
to our physical state of being with
an attitude toward improvement or
positively accommodating for
freedom and independence is
empowering. Reacting negatively
is destructive, crippling, and powerless.*

J R Curtin [8]

What is health?

It seems that even more problematic than defining what constitutes a *disease* is what constitutes health. In *The Short Reign of Pippin IV,* [9] John Steinbeck wrote: *"Pippin was healthy in so far as he knew – by that I mean his health was so good he was not aware he had it."* In 1946, The World Health Organisation arrived at a definition which attempted to avoid the link between health and *disease.* Health is the "state of complete physical, mental and social wellbeing". This seems a high ideal and very few people would consider themselves healthy using that definition. Indeed, a prominent physician's comment on the WHO definition was that he had only known this state in people who are manic or about to have a heart attack! Could we define health by how long we live, or how happy we are or by how many times we have visited our doctor?

How do ordinary people describe health? These are some definitions taken from a French study:

My body functions like a well-oiled machine without having to be looked after – and there's also having sparkling eyes, a good colour, feeling at ease when you meet friends and not being on edge.

I feel strong, able to make an effort, able to keep awake, on top, not tired, not aware of my weakness. [10]

Another Frenchman describing how he feels when he is healthy says:

It's able to act so as to do what you want to do, live how you want to live. [11]

It seems that "healthiness" can, at times, be equated to "robustness" or "hardiness" – how much one *can do* and how one copes with the stresses of daily living. On the other hand, health can also be equated to *how one feels, one's mental attitude and stage of contentment*. To define health, it is necessary to know in what context and in what culture the person is living. A more accurate concept may be arrived at if the phrase *comparative health* is used. This suggests that standards of "healthiness" vary from country to country. Yet another concept is that of *acceptable health*. Such a definition has been provided by Williamson, who writes:

> *Acceptable health is a state of perceived well-being whether or not disease or disability is present, provided that the latter does not interfere either with the sufferer's normal life or with that of people whom he or she may affect through community living.* [12]

This interest in health and healthy activities is partly the result of the social and economic changes of Western countries that have occurred within the last fifty years. These changes have brought with them their own particular form of *diseases*. No longer are we having to deal with the problem of infection and malnutrition, but with the conditions of heart disease, arthritis and cancer. Many of these diseases are multifactorial in origin and do not lend themselves to the "magic bullet" approach to treatment. Some of the factors involved relate to life-style — patterns of exercise and relaxation, diet and dietary imbalances — as opposed to malnutrition and bacterial infection. In addition, we have witnessed an epidemic of disorders of mood and desire, so that, increasingly, the role of the healthcare practitioner has had to involve health education and behavioural modifications.

The response from the professional healthcare practitioners has been slow and there has been a dramatic increase in the involvement of what can be labelled as the "popular health movement". The emphasis on lifestyle changes is not new and Hippocrates himself was aware of its limitation when he wrote:

> *When a carpenter is ill he asks the physician for a rough and ready cure, an emetic or a purge or cautery or the knife, these are his remedies. And if someone prescribes for him a course of dietetics [diet] and exercise and that he must swathe and swaddle his head, and all that sort of thing, he replies at once that he has not time to be ill and that he sees no good of a life spent in nursing his disease to the neglect of his customary employment.* [13]

It is clear that Hippocrates felt that health maintenance programmes and lifestyle advice were only for the affluent. The modern explosion of interest in these areas seems to support his original observation.

Sylvester Graham, a Pennsylvanian temperance lecturer in the early part of the nineteenth century, founded a movement (Grahamism), the basis of which was the advocacy of vegetarianism, bathing, fresh air, sunlight, dress reform, sex hygiene and abstention from drink. *The Graham Journal*, or *The Health Journal Advocate,* [14] published during this lifetime, could be viewed as the precursor of the myriad of similar publications that can be found in any store selling magazines today. Other journals and societies followed – *The Ladies Physiological Reform Society* and *The Physiology of Marriage* being two typical titles. The movement was so strong that the laws against quackery, "*the irregular practice of medicine*", were revoked. In England, similar movements linked to evangelical and social movements developed and in 1828 *The Constitution of Man* was published, a treatise on phrenology and its link to health. The movements were often linked to women's rights and, during the early part of the twentieth century, books on marriage, contraception and natural childbirth began to appear, partly as medical books, but partly as socio-political treatises. The era of scientific medicine, with the advances in surgery, pharmacology and anaesthesia, threatened to overwhelm the popular health movement and make its message redundant. For like Hippocrates' carpenter, most people would prefer to take the magic bullet rather than worry about their food, exercise patterns or attitudes. The modern resurgence of this popular movement occurred in the Sixties and, as on previous occasions, it was linked to feminist and political issues. *Our Bodies, Ourselves* [15] was an immediate bestseller and, like Graham's book in the 1820s, heralded a series of similar books, magazines, periodicals, health clubs and jogging groups.

The importance of food in the maintenance of health has had an impact on the health food industry where now almost every major supermarket has a health food aisle whereas, previously, the purchase of such items was possible only at specialised food stores. Both the popular health movement and the health food industry have become permanent features in our national life, and together with the growth and interest in alternative and complementary therapies form part of the move away from traditional medical-orientated and disease-based models of healthcare practice.

COMPASSION AND THE DELIVERY OF HEALTHCARE IN PRIMARY CARE

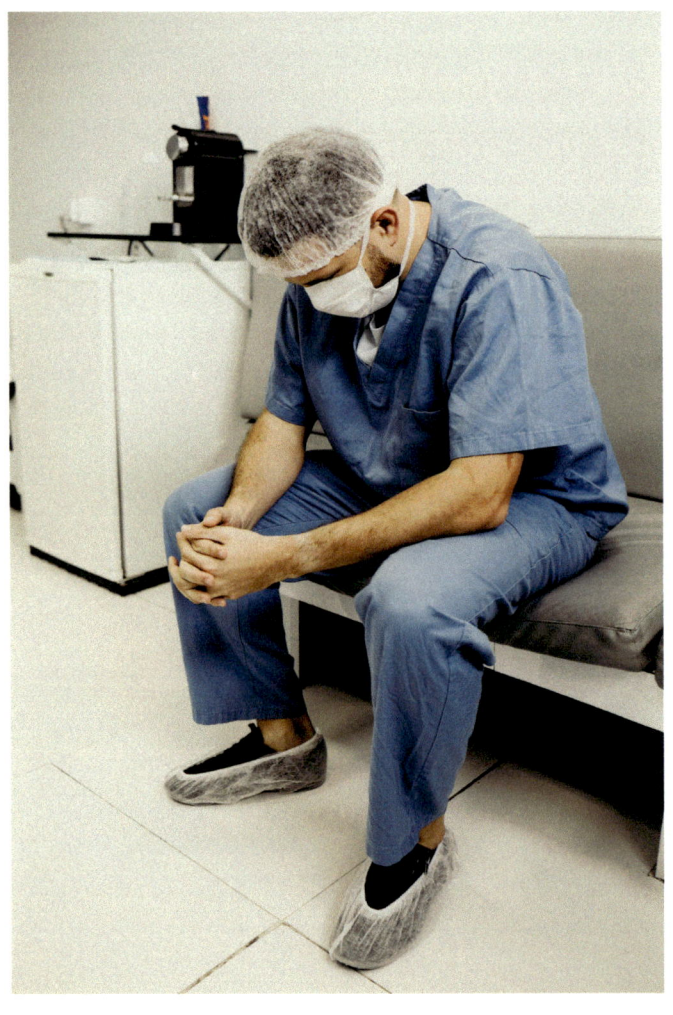

DOCTORS

Man dies too soon, beside his works half-planned.
    His days are counted and reprieve is vain:
    Who shall entreat with Death to stay his hand;
Or cloke the shameful nakedness of pain?

Send here the bold, the seekers of the way –
    The passionless, the unshakeable of soul,
Who serve the inmost mysteries of man's clay,
    And ask no more than leave to make them whole.

Rudyard Kipling [16]

I have limited myself to describing the encounter patients have with their general practitioner (UK) or primary care physician/ Family Doctor (US). It is nevertheless true that the issues raised by compassionate healthcare delivery apply to hospital medicine as well. Although many of the examples and descriptions will be from my own experience as a general practitioner in the UK, the research that underpins much of what I describe came from a three-year study I undertook when I was Family Practice Residency Director in the University of Cincinnati, Ohio (US). [17] Let me start with a few quotes from the foreword in the book *Compassion, Continuity and Caring in the NHS* [18] published by the Royal College of General Practitioners, whose motto is *cum scientia caritas*.

> *So if compassion is so central, why is it not the guaranteed norm in every single encounter with health care? Patients want and deserve to be treated with respect, dignity and compassion. Sometimes they experience care that is impersonally focused on the task, rather than the human being. We need to understand why that is.*
>
> *On top of this there is the whole issue of our sheer busyness. It is extraordinarily difficult to be compassionate when the pressures on you are overwhelming. Exhaustion can so easily be dehumanizing. And even the finest doctor can feel overwhelmed. The more caring the doctor, the more the risk of compassion fatigue.*
>
> *So what is to be done? We can start by valuing compassion, and care, and dignity. Everyone with any influence on the healthcare system has to recognise the absolute essential importance of these aspects of care. This isn't to denigrate the*

technical and the biomedical. It is to recognise the fact that these are synergistic – we absolutely need both. [19]

The motto *cum scientia caritas* can roughly be translated *"science with caring"*. Following the Royal College of General Practitioners inquiry into *Patient Centered Care in the Twenty First Century* [20] it concluded,

> *An inevitable consequence of change throughout the NHS will be the re-negotiation of the doctor-patient contract. The traditional paternalistic model of the patient giving up control to experts in exchange for medical care and professionalism no longer fits with the burden of illness the NHS is treating. Chronic disease management lends itself to greater patient autonomy, self-care and personal responsibility for health. Thus a new agenda that involves substantial empowerment of the patient needs to be embraced, not feared, by healthcare professionals. An NHS that can evolve to adopt this shift will thrive and survive; an NHS that clings to faded glories is destined for the museum.* [21]

A good doctor's comforting and reassuring words are sometimes more powerful than medicines.

We shall examine what compassion looks like:

1. In the consulting room between doctor and patient

    Spiritual intervention for arthritic knees

    An elderly Bangladeshi man came to see me with painful knees. The examinations indicated he had mild arthritis and I prescribed some cream to rub on the knees. He re turned the following week and asked for an x-ray which showed he had mild arthritis. The following week when he returned asking for a specialist referral I asked him, "Do you have difficulty when you pray?" His face lit up and he said, "My wife died last month and I go to the mosque to pray and be with her, but it becomes too painful." I suggested I would phone the senior Muslim Director of the mosque and suggest he be allowed to sit and pray in the mosque. This was agreed and he returned (with presents) to thank me.

2. The responsiveness of the practice, health centre, doctor, and office to the patient's request

    Who is the patient and what is the problem?

    A young mother brought her four year old boy to see me with what appeared to be a minor cold. He looked unhappy, as did the mother who requested antibiotics. I examined the child and noted his chest and lungs were clear. I asked the mother why she decided to bring him to the doctor. She said, "My husband is on night work and came home and heard Jimmy cry and cough. He shouted at me, "Take him to the doctor today. How can I sleep with him coughing? You must look after him better than you have." She then burst into tears.

    Clearly the problem was not with the child, who was by now clutching his mother, but with the marriage.

3. How the "patient journey" from the primary care center to the hospital to homecare is managed

    Avoiding over-prescribing

    Requests for antibiotics for children or adults with colds and coughs is very common. Usually, my response is, "If you take antibiotics you will get better in a week. If you don't take antibiotics you will get better in seven days."

However, I add, "I will give you a prescription, but don't take it to the pharmacy. Wait for two-three days and if you are not better then take the prescription to the chemist." My follow-up to this practice revealed that only one out of ten prescriptions are taken to the chemist, and I suspect very few courses of treatment are completed.

4. What care and support in the community is organised to respond to the patient's needs

Learning from experience

Following morning surgery the GPs (six) would meet to discuss and share our home visits. We had a young trainee doctor with us, and I asked him to visit "Mrs Smith" whose husband had just died. He looked at me askance and said, "What can I do? He is dead." I suggested he go. He reported back that Mrs. Smith had welcomed him, offered him a cup of tea and spent five minutes thanking him for coming and thanking the "good doctors and nurses" at the practice who had looked after her husband. After five-ten minutes when the doctor had said nothing, she said, "You are very kind to have come, but I have kept you too long talking and you must be very busy." The doctor left without saying anything, not examining her, and not prescribing.

Twenty years later, I received a letter from the not-so-young doctor, who wrote and said, "Patrick, that visit you sent me on taught me what being a doctor in the community is all about."

5. Doctor practicing self-compassion

Practicing self-compassion

A young 20 year old single woman came in requesting an abortion. My wife had just had her second ectopic and we knew we would never have children together. I could feel my eyes about to burst into tears, and I said, "I have no problem with your request, but I would prefer if you see my colleague next door who will help you". (I did not explain to her why I could not continue with the consultation).

I see these five stages as underpinning my own ideal model of healthcare delivery – community oriented primary healthcare.

COMMUNITY ORIENTED PRIMARY HEALTHCARE

The Consultation

The research I undertook in Cincinnati attempted to answer the
question: Why do some patients leaving the doctor's office will
be heard to say, "He/she was a very good doctor and listened to
me", or the opposite, "I don't think he listened to what I had to
say". I set up a doctor's office with a two-way window and filmed
many consultations. I then asked three series of "judges" to rate
the consultation as to whether the Doctor exhibited a compassion-
ate approach to the patient (the three sets of judges were experi-
enced family doctors, psychologists and other patients). I collected
the "top ten" consultations as rated by the judges and went frame
by frame examining whether there were any shared behaviours
(you can read a summary of my full report in *Language and*

Communication in General Practice [22]). In summary, we found that in those consultations that were rated highly on the following attributes – good rapport, sensitivity, empathetic listening, compassionate understanding – the doctors exhibited similar "non-verbal" behaviours which were common to all of them.

Non-verbal communication is the process whereby we transmit messages without words. It can be vocal, as when the doctor reinforces patient dialogue with the appropriate "uh-uh" or non-vocal, which encompasses the use of facial expression, body postures, gestures, head nods and so on. Edward Sapir, a pioneer in the field of language, wrote:

> *We respond to gestures with an extreme alertness, and one might say, in accordance with an elaborate and secret code that is written by no-one, known by no-one and understood by all.* [23]

Ray Birdwhistell, an anthropologist who has studied non-verbal behaviour, calculated that in a normal two-person conversation the verbal component carries less than 35 per cent of the social meaning of the situation and *more than 65 per cent is carried by the non-verbal components.*[24] in other words, what we usually call the *rapport* between two people is more linked to the degree of *non-verbal sensitivity* between them than to the words they utter.

I have used the two consultations scripted below to illustrate the significance of the non-verbal signals that can accompany the verbal content. So, in both consultations the verbal content remains the same, whereas the non-verbal exchange between doctor and patient are very different.

Consultation 1

Scene. *Consulting room with doctor (D) sitting behind a big desk with chair available for patient (P) directly opposite.*

D Do sit down. *(Fumbles through notes on desk, looks up eventually after writing something in notes. Middle-aged female patient walks in, dressed in smart, brightly coloured clothes.)*

D Er ... um ... Mrs. Ackerman, isn't it?

P Yes. *(Sits on chair at opposite side of desk.)*

D Well, what can I do for you? *(Still arranging notes, using short, sharp, quick words.)*

P I have come for my prescription.

D *(Looks through notes again. Pauses.)* Yes, I see ... Now what is it you are on? *(Looks through notes again.)* Oh, yes, of course ... the little yellow tablets ... *(Takes out prescription pad and starts writing.)*

P Doctor, ... I have been getting ... these headaches lately. *(Patient leans forward hesitantly, attempting to engage doctor, who is writing and not looking at her.)*

D Uh-um! What are they like? *(Taps desk with pencil.)*

P Well, I have had them before ... and my previous doctor said they were migraine ... but I am getting them all the time now ... and I can't sleep very well ... and another thing ... Doctor, I would like to stop the pill. *(During this, doctor is fidgeting in his chair and scratching his head. He glances quickly at his watch.)*

D *(Briskly.)* Well! Which of these would you like me to deal with first? *(Irritation and emphasis places on "Well".)*

P   Well, doctor, my husband says that it must be the pill that is causing all this trouble ... I get so depressed sometimes ... *(Patient looks down and slumps back into chair.)*

D   Do you sometimes feel like crying? *(Head up. Looking at patient for the first time. As she is about to cry, he raises his hand.)* It does you good to have a cry sometimes, you know. *(Telephone rings.)*
(Doctor leans back in his chair and engages in conversation on the telephone, smiling and muttering enquiringly. Takes out diary, looks through it – glances occasionally at patient and finally turns back to her, as he winds up the phone call.)

D   Look, I can't talk to you now – I'll ring you back later. *(Looks at notes again.)*

D   Sorry, Mrs. Ackerman. Do go on.

P   *(Moving to edge of chair as if about to get up.)* Well, maybe, Doctor, I should come when you are less busy.

D   *(Getting up as he speaks.)* Well, I think you ought to come and talk to me a bit more.

Consultation 2

Scene. *Consulting room with doctor (D) sitting at the edge of his desk with chair available for patient (P) at the side. Patient enters. Doctor half gets out of seat, pointing at chair for patient. Draws his own chair round the desk, using a soft enquiring voice and looking directly at patient.*

D   Do sit down. Mrs. Ackerman isn't it? *(Smiles and makes eye contact.)*

P   Yes. *(Smiles nervously back.)*

D   Well, what can I do for you? *(Looking at her and leaning forward in chair.)*

P   I have come for my prescription.

D   Yes, I see. Now what is it you are on? Oh, yes, of course, the little yellow tablets. *(Doctor leans a bit more forward.)*

P   Doctor, … I have been getting … these headaches lately.

D   Um! What are they like?

P   Well, Doctor … I've had them before and my previous doctor said they were migraine … but, I am getting them all the time now … and I can't sleep very well … and another thing, Doctor, I would like to stop the pill.

D   *(Doctor has stayed leaning forward and does not take his eyes off patient. Pauses – smiles, sits back in his chair.)* Which of these would you like me to deal with first?

P   Well, Doctor, my husband says that it must be the pill that is causing all this trouble … I get so depressed sometimes …

D   *(Leans forward and nods head.)* Do you sometimes feel like crying? *(Doctor leans forward further and touches patient's hand. She begins to cry. Doctor does not move and waits a while before passing her some tissues. Pauses again.)* *(Telephone rings.)*

D   (*Answers the phone, but stops conversation before it has begun.*) Look, I can't talk to you now, I'll ring back later. Sorry, Mrs Ackerman. Do go on.

P   Well maybe, Doctor, I should come when you are less busy?

D   Well, I think we should talk a bit more …

What I learnt during the course of this research is just how much knowledge pertinent to the work of a doctor is available from other academic disciplines which is never referred to in the current medical school training. My research led me to study in greater depth the field of non-verbal communication, etc.

Proxemics. The study of space, time, position and artifacts as part of a dynamic communication process.

Kinesics. The study of facial expression, body posture, hand gestures.

Paralanguage. The study of vocal emphasis and intonation as communication.

Touch. The study of how, when and why touch is employed as part of the communication process.

The findings of our research identified four constant aspects of the Doctors' non-verbal behaviour that contributed to their consultation with the patient as "sensitive", good listener, compassionate, etc. These were:

1.   Good eye contact
2.   Did not sit behind the desk (did not look at the computer)
3.   Spoke at the same rate as the patient
4.   Used touch when seemed appropriate

One unexpected observation was when we "fast-forwarded"
the video the doctor and patient seemed to be "performing a
dance", which is now labelled "attunement", and is also ob-
served when a mother breast/bottle feeds her baby. Com-
passion is, amongst other things, the ability to "tune into" the
other person(s) one is in contact with.

The responsiveness of the practice/doctor's office

In the last 20 years in the UK, "market forces" have been at
work in helping to shape the relationship between the individ-
ual patient and the doctor. The provision of "medical services"
is now framed by the supply and demand of the market.

Health economists have identified what the customer/consumer
patient is seeking from the healthcare centre.

- Availability – the relationship between available services and the volume of patients and their needs
- Accessibility – the relationship between the location of the point of care and the means of patients to get there
- Accommodation – the relationship between the operational set-up of the practice and the patient's perception of appropriateness of the provision
- Affordability – the relationship between the cost of care and the ability of patients to pay for that care. At present this is not such a problem for actual health provision in the UK, but transport costs, non-NHS fees and prescription surcharges can significantly limit a patient's ability to access appropriate health care.
- Acceptability – the relationship between a patient's perception of his or her healthcare providers, and – just as important – the healthcare provider's perception of their clients.[25]

In our own health centre (see The Marylebone Experiment[26]) we introduced the following protocols:

a. Telephone is answered within three rings.
b. Patients can talk to a doctor on the phone between 11:00-12:00 am.
c. Each doctor acts as receptionist for a half-day every week.
d. Five "emergency appointments" are available every day.
e. Home visits are undertaken daily on request, and people over 75 who are not able to come to the practice are visited once every three months.
f. Informal complaints systems were established by the practice and overseen by lawyers/solicitors/attorneys who were registered with the practice (see the Marylebone Experiment [26]).

THE MARYLEBONE CENTRE TRUST
PATRON HRH THE PRINCE OF WALES

g. Additional services provided by extended primary
    healthcare team
    - Direct appointments with practice nurse
    - One-to-one counselling service
    - Massage therapy sessions
    - Self-help and stress management classes
    - Health visitor available for children under five

Innovation in Community Care and Primary Health

The Marylebone Experiment

Edited by
PATRICK PIETRONI
CHRISTOPHER PIETRONI

Foreword by
KEN CALMAN

Community Care and Primary Health
University of Westminster

CHURCHILL
LIVINGSTONE

The Marylebone Health Centre has for over ten years pioneered an integrated approach to health care within the National Health Service. The Centre offers its patients a wide range of additional complementary therapies as well as a comprhensive educational programme of self-help classes. The community Outreach work addresses the needs of the isolated and more vulnerable members of the Community.

Since I opened the Centre in 1986 many other such units have now followed the 'Marylebone Model'. I am very keen that this important work is continued and am delighted that the Centre is now expanding its activities. Clearly, it would be wonderful to have the necessary support to permit the expansion of the Centre in the Crype of Marylebone Church and I much look forward to opening the new Centre early next year.

HDRH Prince Charles

Outreach and Community Care

Traditionally, general practice has been a "reactive service" ie appointments to see the doctor are instigated by the patient. In the Marylebone Experiment we introduced an outreach service after identifying our most isolated and vulnerable patients. This included those aged over 75, refugees living in bed and breakfast hotels and patients with long-term chronic conditions who required "daily care" and help with bathing. In addition, we established a patient volunteer programme which was overseen by a staff member, but supported by the voluntary involvement of members of our registered patients.

Community care programmes at the Marylebone Health Centre

1. Transport service for patients and their relatives
2. Decorating and minor repair services
3. Befriending (sitting with elderly patients)
4. Telephone contact—once a month for all over 75
5. Single parents club
6. Newsletter three times per year
7. Language interpreter service
8. Homelss accomodation service (we have a large population of refugee patients)
9. Crisis listening service (drop-in)
10. Swimming club
11. Movement to music
12. Choir singing
13. Elderly-toddler afternoons
14. Yoga classes
15. Reminiscence group

Percentage of patients completing the questionnaire (n=479), who offered help or needed help for the tasks listed

	% offering Help	% requesting Help
Listening/befriending	31.52	8.98
Shopping/errands	14.61	3.76
Legal advice	0.84	7.93
Transporting in car	5.64	2.51
Housing advice	1.04	6.05
Babysitting	7.72	4.95
Job/career advice	5.43	5.85
Childminding	6.26	4.38
Social security advice	0.46	3.97
Sitting with frail adults	8.56	1.04
Language interpreting	8.98	2.71
Decorating	5.43	3.13
Literacy	10.86	0.63
Letter writing	20.46	3.34

Much learning occurred for all of us involved in The Marylebone Experiment. The most important lesson for me was that acting compassionately, organising, facilitating and encouraging compassionate behaviour and action can be achieved without necessarily *feeling* compassionate yourself.

Fairness and justice in a community looks like what private and individual acts of compassion look like in public.

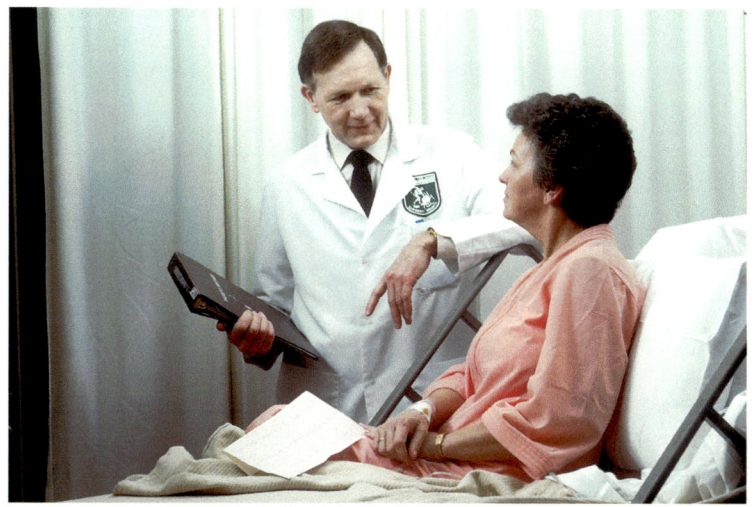

The Patient Journey In and Out of Hospital

Referring patients for further investigation, specialist opinion
and admission to hospital is not an infrequent task undertaken
by the primary care doctor. We instigated evening meetings
with our hospital specialist colleagues and explored how the
"journey" from the primary care doctors to the hospital could
be enabled to reduce stress, concern and confusion for the
patient. With the advent of the computer information can now
be rapidly transmitted between doctor and doctor. We did
introduce the sending of a letter to the patient to ensure they
were also informed. We encouraged the primary care physician
to find time to visit his/her patient once they had been admitted
to hospital.

FINALLY

A SHROPSHIRE LAD: II – LOVELIEST OF TREES, THE CHERRY NOW

Loveliest of trees, the cherry now
Is hung with bloom along the bough,
And stands about the woodland ride
Wearing white for Eastertide.

Now, of my threescore years and ten,
Twenty will not come again,
And take from seventy springs a score,
It only leaves me fifty more.

And since to look at things in bloom
Fifty springs are little room,
About the woodlands I will go
To see the cherry hung with snow.

A E Housman [27]

COMPASSION WITHIN HEALTHCARE SETTINGS

The Royal College of Psychiatrists (UK) published a faculty report in 2015 entitled *Compassion in care: ten things you can do to make a difference.*[28] In the introduction they wrote:

> *The purpose of this faculty report is to highlight why compassion is important, what gets in the way of delivering compassionate care and what can be done to facilitate it. The intended audience is primarily psychiatrists, but the actions identified to encourage compassionate care can apply to all health and social care professionals in any care setting.*

I would also add that the following list could apply to many other work settings:

> *How to demonstrate compassion: ten things you can do every day*

1. *Be alive to your internal world – your capacity to tolerate distress, your emotional state and your level of fatigue – and take measures to maintain resilience or improve matters if needed.*
2. *Support the development of systems at work that give you and your colleagues a space to reflect on what you are doing, and attend those events when they happen.*
3. *Remember that patients are usually in distress – that is why they are in your care. Treat them as people, not diagnoses. Remember the importance of basic communication and interview skills: intelligent listening, mindfulness with regard to dynamics, proper interview setting.*

4. *Model compassionate behaviour for trainees and other members of staff. Like it or not, you work in a complex system, and how you are affects others around you.*
5. *If there is system problem, do not work around it or ignore it. Addressing it is your duty, and in the end it is better for you, your colleagues and your patients. Remember, the standard you walk by is the standard you accept.*
6. *If there is a problem with someone else's behaviour or attitude, challenge it appropriately. Although this is difficult, it is essential and again better for you, your colleagues and your patients.*
7. *Make sure training activities foster the right behaviour and values among trainees.*
8. *Respect systems, but think of people and relationships. It is people who get things done, not forms on a computer. Go see someone rather than call. Call rather than email. Foster good working relationships. Make tea. And do the washing up.*
9. *Make the patient in front of you your primary concern, while balancing that attention with other commitments that you and the organization might have to other patients.*
10. *Pay attention and be respectful. When in consultations or meetings, turn phones and tablets off. Be in the situation, not somewhere else. And when your business is done, leave. Your time and energy are limited, and so are those of others.*

Compassion can involve
Thinking, Feeling and Acting

One can think compassionately without feeling compassionate.

One can act compassionately without thinking compassionately.

One can feel compassionately without acting compassionately.

How much more could be achieved if these issues formed part of the training of our future doctors.

References

1. Urquhart, H. (1974). *My mind lets go a thousand things.* Unpublished.

2. Clough, A. H. (2016). *Say not the struggle nought availeth.* Available at www.poetryfoundation.org/poems/43959/say-not-the-struggle-nought-availeth. Last accessed December 2020.

3. Pietroni, P. (1990). *The Greening of Medicine.* London. Gollancz.

4. Pietroni, P. (1990). *ibid.*

5. Pietroni, P. (1990). *op.cit.*

6. Pietroni, P. (1990). *op.cit.*

7. Pietroni, P. (1990). *op.cit.*

8. Curtin, J. R. (2020). On Civility. Louisville. Old Stone Press.

9. Pietroni, P. (1990). *op.cit.*

10. Cassileth, B. R. (1982). After Laetrile, What? *New England Journal of Medicine.* 306:1482-1484.

11. Cassileth, B. R. (1982). *ibid.*

12. Williamson, J. D. & Danaher, K. (1978). *Self-Care in Health.* London. Croom Helm.

13. Pietroni, P. (1990). *op.cit.*

14. Graham, S. (1839). *Lectures in the Science of Human Life.* Boston. Marsh, Capen, Lyon & Webb.

15. Boston Women's Collective. (1975). *Our Bodies, Ourselves.* London. Simon & Schuster.

16. Kipling, R. (1994). *Collected Poems of Rudyard Kipling.* Ware. Wordsworth Editions.

17. Tanner, B. (Ed.). (1976). *Language and Communication in General Practice.* London. Hodder & Stoughton.

18. Charlton, R. (2016). *Compassion, Continuity and Caring in the NHS.* London. Royal College of General Practitioners.

19. Charlton, R. (2016). *ibid.*

20. Royal College of General Practitioners. (2014). *Inquiry into Patient Centered Care in the 21st Century.* Available at Inquiry into Patient Centred Care in the 21st Century (rcgp.org.uk). Last accessed December 2020.

21. Royal College of General Practitioners. (2014). *ibid*

22. Tanner, B. (Ed.). (1976). *op.cit.*

23. Sapir, E. (1966). *Culture, Language and Personality.* University of California Press.

24. Birdwhistell, R. L. (1970). *Kinesics and Context: Essays on Body Motion Communication.* University of Pennsylvania Press.

25. White, K.L., Franklin Williams, T., Greenberg, B.G. (1961). *The Ecology of Medical Care.* The New England Journal of Medicine: 265. pp. 885-892.

26. Pietroni, P. & Pietroni, C. (1996). *Innovation in Community Care and Primary Health: The Marylebone Experiment.* London. Churchill Livingstone.

27. Housman, A. E. (1896). *A Shropshire Lad: II: Loveliest of trees, the cherry now.* Available at https://poetryarchive.org/poem/shropshire-lad-ii-loveliest-trees-cherry-now/. Last accessed December 2020.

28. The Royal College of Psychiatrists. (2015). *Compassion in care: ten things you can do to make a difference.* Available at www.rcpsych.ac.uk/docs/default-source/members/faculties/general-adult-psychiatry/general-adult-fr-gap-02-compassionate-care.pdf?sfvrsn=e6852ee1_2 Last accessed December 2020.

Image Credits

Image 1   Testing for Covid. Jakayla Toney from Unsplash. Page 8.
Image 2   Pietroni, P. (1990). *The Greening of Medicine*. London.
           Gollancz. Page 9.
Image 3   Comparison of relationship between primary and secondary
           systems from Pietroni, P. (1990). *The Greening of Medicine*.
           London. Gollancz. Page 9.
Image 4   What people do about their symptoms from Pietroni, P. (1990).
           The Greening of Medicine. London. Gollancz. Page 10.
Image 5   Cogito Ergo Sum. Shutterstock. Page 12.
Image 6   Hospital staff in scrubs. Jonathan Borba from Pexels. Page 22.
Image 7   "A good doctor's comforting and reassuring words .."
           https://wishesmessages.com/thank-you-messages-for-doctors-
           thank-you-notes-for-doctors/. Page 26.
Image 8   Patient and Doctor.
           www.washingtonpost.com/news/wonk/wp/2015/09/16/how-
           the-doctor-patient-relationship-has-become-a-prisoners-
           dilemma/). Page 30.
Image 9   Communication. University of Malaya, Kuala Lumpur. Page 36.
Image 10   Marylebone Health Centre Appeal image. Page 38.
Image 11   Work undertaken at the Marylebone Centre. Pietroni, P. &
           Pietroni, C. (1996). *Innovation in Community Care and
           Primary Health: The Marylebone Experiment*. London.
           Churchill Livingstone. Page 39.

Image 12 Letter from HRH Prince Charles, Patron of the Marylebone Centre. Page 40.

Image 13 Photograph taken on an annual visit of the Patron, HRH Prince Charles with Professor Patrick Pietroni. Page 40.

Image 14 Pietroni, P. & Pietroni, C. (1996). *op.cit.* Page 41.

Image 15 Pietroni, P. & Pietroni, C. (1996). *op.cit.* Page 42.

Image 16 Doctor with patient in hospital. National Cancer Institute. Page 43.

Image 17 Doctor vaccinating young boy. National Cancer Institute from Unsplash. Page 47.

Publisher
SF Design, llc / Fresco Books
Albuquerque, New Mexico
frescobooks.com

ISBN: 978-1-934491-81-2